DATE DUE

TEEN MENTAL HEALTH™

ADD and ADHD

Therese Shea

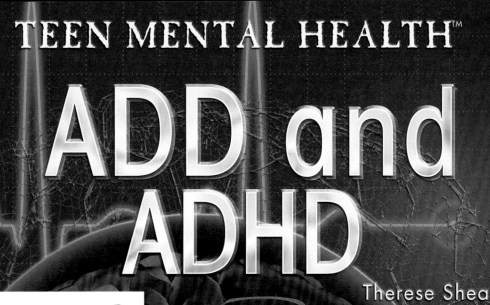

ROSEN
PUBLISHING®

New York

Published in 2014 by The Rosen Publishing Group, Inc.
29 East 21st Street, New York, NY 10010

Library of Congress Cataloging-in-Publication Data

Shea, Therese.
ADD and ADHD/Therese Shea.–First edition.
        pages cm–(Teen mental health)
Includes bibliographical references and index.
ISBN 978-1-4777-1749-3 (library binding)
1. Attention-deficit hyperactivity disorder–Juvenile literature.
2. Attention-deficit disorder in adults–Juvenile literature. I. Title.
RJ506.H9S535 2014
618.92'8589–dc23

                                        2013012403

Manufactured in the United States of America

CPSIA Compliance Information: Batch #W14YA: For further information, contact Rosen Publishing, New York, New York, at 1-800-237-9932.

ADD and ADHD

contents

chapter one   What Are ADD and ADHD?   **4**

chapter two   The Symptoms of ADHD **11**

chapter three   Getting Help **19**

chapter four   Medications **27**

chapter five   Living Well with ADHD **35**

glossary **41**

for more information **43**

for further reading **45**

index **47**

chapter one

What Are ADD and ADHD?

ADD and ADHD are two abbreviations tossed around in the media, in schools, and in everyday life. You probably already know the terms are used to label, often wrongly, young people who do not pay attention or cannot sit still in class. Everyone feels distracted, impulsive, or excited sometimes. These are not indications of ADD or ADHD.

ADD and ADHD are disorders, meaning they are conditions that have a deeply negative effect on a person's life. Specifically, ADD and

People who suffer from ADD or ADHD may simply appear withdrawn and not necessarily exhibit symptoms that others can see.

ADHD are neurobehavioral disorders. That means the behaviors exhibited as a result of the disorders—such as the inability to concentrate, stay focused, and ignore distractions—can be traced to neurons in the parts of the brain that control these abilities. ADHD may also be categorized as a neurodevelopmental disorder, as it impairs the growth and development of neurons.

ADHD stands for attention deficit/hyperactivity disorder. The definition of the disorder has been changed and amended many times, but the basic symptoms remain:

inattention, impulsivity, and hyperactivity. ADD stands for attention deficit disorder. This term is sometimes used interchangeably with ADHD, but it is actually a type of ADHD that does not include hyperactive behaviors.

Some people think ADHD is a new condition, but only the label is new. The first medical record of children exhibiting the combination of inattentiveness, impulsiveness, and hyperactivity was in 1902. Since then, ADHD has been given many different names, including minimal brain dysfunction, restlessness syndrome, and hyperkinetic disorder.

ADHD can be hard to diagnose because it does not have clearly defined markers or symptoms as a disease or illness like cancer and chicken pox have. For that reason, some people do not believe ADHD is a real disorder. However, many accepted disorders, including manic depression and schizophrenia, cannot be diagnosed by a blood test or another definitive examination. Few would argue these are not actual mental ailments. Most professionals agree that ADHD is a legitimate neurobehavioral disorder.

One reason ADHD is on the minds and lips

Hyperactivity is just one of the symptoms of ADHD. Hyperactivity is not just another name for being energetic. It is an abnormal restlessness and desire to be active.

of so many people is its prevalence. According to a recent household survey by the U.S. Centers for Disease Control and Prevention (CDC), 9 percent of all American children ages three to seventeen have been diagnosed with ADHD. That is more than five million young people. Some estimates are even higher.

According to a recent Northwestern Medicine study using reports from doctors' offices, 10.4 million people under age 18 were diagnosed with ADHD at physician visits over the course of one year recently, compared with 6.2 million a decade before. Past estimates of ADHD occurrence were lower than those of today, some as low as 3 percent. Is it more common today? No, it is more likely that awareness of the disorder and its symptoms have led to more people being tested for it. Interestingly, ADHD is more commonly found in boys, who are about twice as likely to be diagnosed with ADHD than girls.

ADHD has been found in every country that has been studied. Prevalence rates have been reported from 1 to 10 percent in Canada, Germany, the Netherlands, New Zealand, Norway, Puerto Rico, and the United Kingdom.

However murky the causes of ADHD are, its impact is powerful. The disorder affects all areas of young people's lives: at home, at school, and in social situations. There are ways of controlling behaviors and managing symptoms so that people can have normal lives. Professionals do not always agree on the type of treatment and how safe those treatments are, specifically medications, so it is important that those affected learn about their disorder and take actions appropriate for their unique condition.

For many, ADHD is not something they outgrow. According to the CDC, about 4 percent of American adults have ADHD. It is not just a childhood disorder. The symptoms diminish with age, so a five-year-old with ADHD and an adult with the same diagnosis will not act alike even in similar situations. The five-year-old may not be able to stop jumping around, while the adult may pace a room. They both feel urges to engage in these hyperactive behaviors. Teenagers and adults may also exhibit impulsiveness by interrupting conversations. They may

Impulsiveness is another characteristic of ADHD. Those with ADHD may not be able to weigh the consequences of their actions as others do.

frequently forget to complete daily activities or have a hard time finishing tasks at work and school. All with ADHD struggle in activities and situations in which those without ADHD often succeed.

ADHD has no cure, so those diagnosed with it need to learn to live with the obstacles of the disorder. People with ADHD are more likely to drop out of school, have car accidents, and lose their job, and they are at greater risk for substance abuse. They may quit or be fired from their workplace because of the far-reaching effects of their condition. They may also see their relationships suffer. That is why it is important to address the possibility of an ADHD diagnosis and learn to manage the disorder. With a wide variety of treatments available, people with ADHD can be successful and happy with their lives.

MYTHS AND FACTS

Myth: ADD and ADHD are new disorders.

Fact: Hippocrates, a Greek doctor who lived from 460 to 370 BCE, wrote about a patient that doctors and researchers now think most likely had ADHD. In the mid-1800s, Heinrich Hoffman, a German doctor, wrote children's books based on some of his patients. He named characters after their symptoms, including Zappel-Philipp (Fidgety Phil).

Myth: Watching television causes ADHD.

Fact: No study has proven a link between watching television and the occurrence of ADHD. In 2004, a report in *Pediatrics* magazine linked television viewing and attention problems. However, it is also possible that kids with inattention problems are more drawn to television viewing than those without.

Myth: Girls are less likely to have ADHD than boys.

Fact: Girls are less likely than boys to be diagnosed with ADHD. According to studies, girls do not have the severe behavior problems that accompany some kinds of ADHD. Therefore, ADHD may just be more difficult to identify in girls. However, girls with ADHD have been noted to have depression, anxiety, low self-esteem, and social, family, and school problems, just as boys with ADHD often have.

chapter two

The Symptoms of ADHD

Most health professionals, including psychologists, psychiatrists, and pediatricians, diagnose attention deficit/hyperactivity disorder based on the occurrence of symptoms outlined in the *Diagnostic and Statistical Manual for Mental Disorders (DSM)*. The manual gives examples of various ways that inattention, hyperactivity, and impulsiveness might be displayed in a person with ADHD. If you have ever babysat a young child, you know that most children exhibit all three of these behaviors at some point. That does not mean the children have ADHD, though. The symptoms must seem inappropriate for someone's age. For example, a ten-year-old should be able to complete a homework assignment and sit still in class. In fact, often the symptoms of ADHD are ignored or misunderstood before a child reaches school age. But once in school, children with ADHD cannot adapt and thrive as their peers do.

Young people with ADHD may notice some differences between themselves and their peers. It may make them feel isolated and the target of abuse.

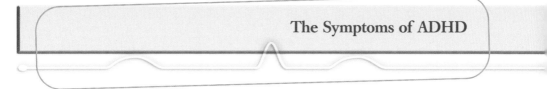

Their symptoms are severe enough to impair their ability to function in the new environment.

The DSM Symptoms

According to the *DSM*, in order for a patient to be diagnosed as having ADHD, he or she must present certain symptoms for at least six months to the degree that he or she cannot function on the same level as a peer. If the behaviors are more recent, it might be a sign that something else is wrong. The patient must show a number of the symptoms under either of the inattention or hyperactivity and impulsivity lists below:

Inattention:

- Often fails to pay attention to details or makes careless mistakes in work or other activities
- Often has difficulty maintaining attention in work or play
- Often does not seem to listen even when spoken to
- Often does not follow instructions and fails to finish work
- Often has trouble organizing work and activities
- Often avoids or dislikes engaging in tasks that require lengthy mental effort
- Often loses things
- Often distracted by unimportant stimuli
- Often forgetful in daily activities

13

Hyperactivity and impulsivity:

- Often fidgets with hands or feet or is restless when seated
- Often leaves seat in situations in which remaining seated is expected
- Often runs or climbs in inappropriate situations
- Often has trouble playing or completing activities quietly
- Often talks excessively
- Is often "on the go" or acts as if "driven by a motor"
- Often has trouble waiting to take turns
- Often yells out answers to questions before they have been completed
- Often interrupts or interferes with others' activities

Patients younger than seventeen must show at least six symptoms in each category for a positive diagnosis. Older patients may exhibit fewer. Even if patients present at least six symptoms in both categories, several other criteria must be met. First, some of the symptoms must have been exhibited by the patient before he or she was twelve years old and to the degree that they impaired daily life. Next, the symptoms must reveal themselves in more than one environment. Also, the degree of impairment must be significant, or serious enough to keep the patient from developing in social, school, and work settings. (Note the word "often" in each of the symptoms.) Finally, the symptoms cannot be traced to any other kind of disorder.

Coexisting Disorders

According to the American Academy of Pediatrics' Committee on Quality Improvement, about one-third of all children with ADHD have at least one other condition. Though it is a challenge for a medical professional to separate the symptoms of ADHD from different disorders, it is an imperative part of the diagnosis process.

Coexisting disorders may need to be addressed and treated in different ways than ADHD. For example, according to the Learning Disabilities Association of America, about 20 to 30 percent of children with ADHD have learning disabilities, such as difficulty understanding words and struggling with certain subjects. Whereas ADHD can be treated with medication, learning disabilities cannot.

Perhaps as many as 40 percent of the ADHD population has oppositional defiant disorder. They are frequently angry, aggressive, and argumentative, and ignore rules. Equally as widespread is conduct disorder, a condition in which people intentionally lie, fight, and engage in high-risk, socially unacceptable behaviors. Medications may help with these disorders, but behavioral therapy and psychotherapy are also needed.

With the stress that ADHD brings, it is no surprise that 10 to 30 percent of young people with ADHD suffer from anxiety and depression. (An even larger percentage of adults with ADHD are diagnosed with these coexisting disorders.) Sometimes those with ADHD have bipolar disorder, which is characterized by long periods of mania followed by depression. The "ups and downs" of this condition make it difficult to participate in life in a normal way.

Tourette syndrome is another ADHD coexisting disorder exemplified by involuntary noises and repetitive movements, such as blinking and twitches. These behaviors can be controlled with medication. More than half of people with Tourette syndrome also have ADHD, though only a small percent of those with ADHD have this condition.

The Causes

The causes of ADHD lie in the brain. Scientists study the areas of the brain that regulate behaviors affected by ADHD. Children with ADHD have thinner tissue in certain areas of the brain than those without ADHD. Scientists have found that this brain tissue becomes thicker as children grow and their symptoms lessen in intensity. Other recent studies comparing the ADHD brain and the non-ADHD brain have suggested young people with ADHD have slightly smaller brain volume than those without. However, those on medication to treat ADHD seemed to have the same brain volume.

What causes these differences in the brain? No one knows for sure, but some common factors exist among those diagnosed with ADHD. Studies suggest

The prevalence of ADHD is constantly inspiring new studies about its causes. Those with ADHD should keep up to date on the latest research.

that mothers who smoked or used alcohol during pregnancy increase the risk their children will have ADHD. These activities have effects on the developing brain. Similarly, there is a link between exposure to lead in paint and plumbing, sometimes found in older buildings, and children under three years old. Just as the toxins in cigarettes, alcohol, and lead can harm the maturing brain, a physical brain injury can lead to ADHD symptoms as well. In particular, damage to the frontal lobe may cause inattentiveness and difficulty controlling impulses. However, this is a rare reason for ADHD.

Heredity is the most common link. Children with ADHD are likely to have a parent or both parents who have ADHD. Geneticists have noticed the brain chemical dopamine is at lower levels in the brains of people with ADHD, so they have focused in on the genes responsible for dopamine. This opens up the possibility of gene therapy in the future.

chapter three

Getting Help

Parents and teachers are often the ones who first recognize the possibility of attention deficit/hyperactivity disorder in young people. They may see them struggling in school, in relationships, and at home. As young people begin puberty, hormones can have an intensifying effect on symptoms, too. Problems with peers, teachers, and authority figures can wreak havoc on academic, family, and social lives.

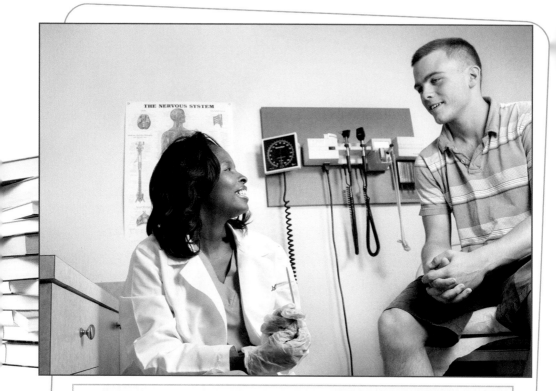

Sometimes a doctor can recognize symptoms of ADHD that a loved one cannot. Patients should always be truthful when answering a doctor's questions.

The first person parents should talk to about suspected ADHD is their family physician. A family doctor can access the patient's history, which is helpful for ruling out other medical conditions that may be affecting him or her. However, most family doctors do not have extensive knowledge of ADHD and so will refer the patient to a more qualified professional for evaluation. This may be a psychiatrist, which is a doctor who specializes in treating conditions that affect brain chemistry and function.

Psychiatrists are knowledgeable about medications, side effects, and ADHD coexisting disorders such as depression and anxiety. A psychologist can also diagnose ADHD but cannot prescribe any needed medication as a psychiatrist can. Typically, more than one professional is involved in the diagnosis and treatment process of ADHD. Other experts on the assessment team may include neurologists, social workers, speech-language pathologists, and learning specialists.

Examination and Testing

Because the symptoms of ADHD are somewhat subjective, it is challenging for even the most knowledgeable professional to diagnose the disorder. A doctor will usually follow several steps before making the diagnosis. First is an interview with the patient so that he or she can answer questions or voice concerns. An interview might also present some of the symptoms in action, such as inattention. Next is a careful review of the patient's medical history, including past issues, family medical history, current prescriptions, and behavior problems at school and home. For example, gifted children may be inattentive in class because they are bored, or inattention can be a sign of a learning disability.

Diet is also considered. Young people who suffer from malnutrition may not function like their peers. This is particularly dangerous for young children whose brains are still developing. Caffeine can lead to hyperactive behaviors as well. Following the medical history is a physical exam in which the patient's hearing, vision, and nervous system responses are tested. He or she is screened for any physical ailments, and other possible disorders are noted.

Rating tests, questionnaires, and surveys have been developed to help in the ADHD diagnosis. These assess physical, mental, and social behaviors. The most common include the Conners Rating Scale; Vanderbilt Assessment Scale; Test of Variables in Attention (TOVA); ADD-H: Comprehensive Teacher Rating Scale (ACTeRS); Barkley Home and School Situations Questionnaire; Behavior Assessment System for Children (BASC); and other checklists that are filled out by both parents and patients.

Besides other conditions, the patient's environments are also examined. Are home and classroom stressful places? Abuse at home or extreme pressure can cause young people to act out. Are teachers or parents mishandling situations and partly the cause of behaviors? The patient needs to be observed in these settings to determine the answer to these questions.

Diagnosis

With comprehensive examinations, medical histories, interviews, tests and questionnaires, and studies of behaviors in multiple settings in hand, the specialist begins to make the diagnosis. He or she tries to rule out any other possible reasons as the cause of the behavior.

If it is determined that ADHD is the cause of the problem, the specialist tries to zero in on the specific symptoms. Patients are often categorized according to whether they are primarily inattentive, are primarily

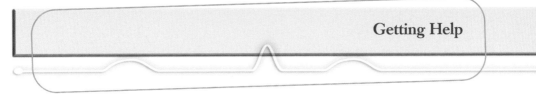

hyperactive and impulsive, or exhibit combined characteristics of all three symptoms in order to treat the most
detrimental elements of ADHD.

Most young people with ADHD have the combined
type. However, in an article on the ADDitude Web site,
David Shaffer, the chief of Columbia University Medical
Center's Division of Child and Adolescent Psychiatry,
said, "Many children who met criteria for a given subtype
at one point, met criteria for a different one a few months
later." This means patients should be reevaluated at least
annually for proper treatment.

Again, since no physical or chemical abnormality can
be detected in patients with ADHD, it is up to the specialist, the patient, and the patient's family to figure out
whether the diagnosis fits. A second or third opinion may
also be sought. After that, the next step is to formulate a
plan for effective management.

Multimodal Treatment

According to the National Resource Center for ADHD,
multimodal treatment is the best approach to attention
deficit/hyperactivity disorder. Multimodal intervention
means employing multiple modes, or methods, of treatment. These include parent and child education about
ADHD, behavioral interventions, educational modifica-
tions, counseling and therapy, and medication if and when
necessary.

First, parents and young people with ADHD must be
knowledgeable about the various symptoms of the condition and its numerous treatments. They must be their

own advocates for addressing problems and seeing that their needs are met.

Additionally, homes can be shaped into affirming, structured environments that are safe havens for those with ADHD. Young people with ADHD often benefit from following a routine. A schedule at home may be posted to observe and prepare for changes to the schedule in advance. Items needed each day should be kept in the same place. Writing down assignments and events is a must.

A counselor can help a family begin successful strategies for living with ADHD. A counselor is trained to observe the family's interactions and suggest healthier ways of communicating.

Behavioral interventions are strategies for changing behavior in challenging situations. Both parents and teachers can enact behavioral interventions. Such tactics include charts, reward systems, and timeouts. Positive behaviors and attributes should be praised to counteract the criticism someone with ADHD may hear about the negative behaviors that accompany the disorder. Even better, people can be coached to praise themselves for controlling ADHD behaviors and using their own interventions.

In school, achievable long-term goals should be set up so that the student with ADHD can succeed in short-term incremental steps. For example, a teacher may recognize that a student needs to stay focused during independent-reading time. The behavioral intervention may be to monitor and reward the student each day that focus is achieved to the best of his or her ability. Note that the intervention does not overreach the achievable goal by asking the student to focus on all schoolwork every day. Instead, it targets a certain behavior at a certain time.

Therapy and counseling are essential parts of multimodal ADHD treatment as well. What's the difference? They are often used interchangeably, but therapy means using a process to treat a problem, while counseling means providing guidance and advice to resolve conflicts and emotional difficulties. Therapists and counselors can coach younger patients in learning to control urges and in reacting to others appropriately, such as reading their facial expressions. They can also help older patients deal with the anxiety and depression that often accompany ADHD.

Special Services

In addition to behavioral interventions at school, it may also be necessary to modify a student's educational plan depending on the severity of ADHD and related problems, with special attention to learning disabilities. Some young people with ADHD may be entitled to services in their schools. In fact, two federal laws may apply.

Section 504 of the Rehabilitation Act of 1973 prohibits discrimination against students with disabilities. In order to qualify, students must be diagnosed with a form of ADHD that considerably affects learning and requires special education or related services, such as a particular seating arrangement or extra time on tests.

The Individuals with Disabilities Education Act (IDEA) guarantees students with disabilities equal access to a good education. This law is not as broad as Section 504. In order for a student to qualify for special education under IDEA, certain criteria must be met: the student should be diagnosed with ADHD by a school-approved professional. The effects of the ADHD must be ongoing and substantially limit educational performance so that special education services are needed.

IDEA mandates eligible students have an Individualized Education Program (IEP)—a course of action that addresses a student's learning problems and details services provided, sets annual goals, and defines how progress is measured. Classroom assistance or technology aids may be required. Parents, teachers, school staff, and students themselves work together to develop an IEP. As they grow older, students should be as involved as possible in setting their goals. The IEP can make it possible for a student with ADHD to excel in school.

chapter four

Medications

Because the cause of ADHD is unknown, there is no cure. However, there are effective treatments. Those with less severe ADHD may benefit from behavioral therapy and other forms of counseling alone. But according to the Centers for Disease Control and Prevention, more than half of children diagnosed with ADHD use medication to control the symptoms.

Medications

Stimulants are the most common types of ADHD medication. While it may seem strange to give a stimulant to an impulsive or hyperactive person, stimulants actually have a calming effect. They reduce both hyperactivity and impulsivity and allow patients to focus. They seem to boost levels of neurotransmitters, which are chemicals that help send messages between nerve cells in the brain. Neurotransmitters stimulate the brain's attention centers. Popular stimulant medications include methylphenidate (brand names: Ritalin, Concerta), dextroamphetamine (brand names: Dexedrine, Dextrostat), and dextroamphetamine-amphetamine (brand name: Adderall). There are many more kinds of stimulants.

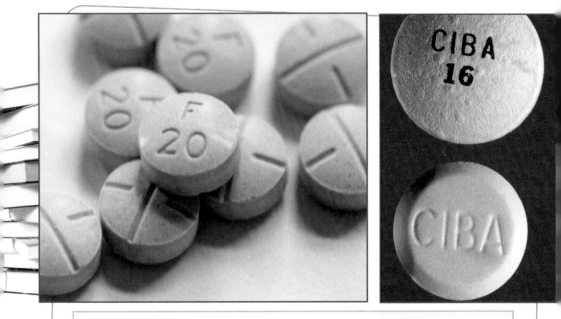

Adderall *(left)* and Ritalin are medications used to treat ADHD. Since they're such powerful drugs, deciding to take them should be carefully considered.

Some patients taking stimulant medications experience uncomfortable side effects, including loss of appetite, irritability, stomachaches, headaches, increased anxiety, and sleep problems. Several medications have been linked to slower growth rates. Effects such as these may disappear in time or with lower doses. If not, different medication may be required.

There are rare side effects associated with stimulants that are especially worrisome. It is thought that patients with preexisting heart conditions have a higher risk of heart attack, stroke, or even death when using stimulants. This is why it is crucial for doctors to review a patient's medical history and perform a full examination before prescribing a stimulant medication. It is rare but possible for patients using stimulants to hear voices, have hallucinations, or become manic. Stimulant use can also lead to addiction without proper management.

Nonstimulant medications have been developed, including atomoxetine (brand name: Strattera), clonidine hydrochloride (brand name: Kapvay), and guanfacine (brand name: Intuniv). One major downside to these is that they are not as effective as stimulants in some patients. In fact, sometimes they are taken with stimulants. While nonstimulants have fewer side effects than stimulants, they are not without problems. Nonstimulant medications may cause nausea, sleepiness, liver problems, and respiratory infections. Most seriously, atomoxetine has been linked to suicidal thoughts in children and teenagers with ADHD.

Antidepressants are an alternative to stimulants and nonstimulants. These include bupropion (brand name: Wellbutrin) and desipramine (brand name: Norpramin). Antidepressants, too, increase levels of neurotransmitters in the brain. They are especially helpful in dealing with the depression and anxiety that accompany ADHD and are nonaddictive. However, they also have their side effects, ranging from dry mouth to seizures. As with all medication, patients need to be monitored carefully.

Once the patient and the caregiver decide on a medication, there are many issues to consider: What form of medication is the patient comfortable with: pill, capsule, liquid, or skin patch? Is the medication long lasting or will the patient need to see the school nurse each day? Depending on the severity of the ADHD, will the patient take medication every day or just on school days? Medications are not something to be taken lightly or without great consideration.

Hyperactivity and impulsiveness seem to lessen with age, so people with ADHD will likely alter treatments as they get older. Medication usually changes in dosage and type. Most professionals agree that medication alone is never sufficient. Young people with ADHD should use coping strategies learned in counseling and therapy and tailor these to their needs as they get older.

Alternative Therapies

Many people look for alternatives to medication for ADHD treatment because of the associated side effects. Along with other parts of the multimodal intervention, exercise has been shown to be an important way of handling some ADHD characteristics. Exercise can help discharge the energy that exhibits itself as restless, fidgety, and unfocused behavior. Like stimulant medications, physical activity releases neurotransmitters in the brain, specifically dopamine, enabling people to give full attention to tasks for extended periods of time. Exercise also combats other problems related to ADHD, such as poor social skills. Being part of a team can help those with ADHD gain self-esteem and learn how to interact appropriately with peers.

Exercise is not just about getting in shape. It benefits all parts of the body—even the brain. It also combats stress and anxiety.

Some people tout natural substances such as gingko biloba and omega-3 fatty acids as alternative therapies, but studies have shown they are not as effective as other medications. Most medical professionals recommend that these be used only under supervision and along with medications, rather than in place of them.

ADHD has been such a mystery in the past that people believed certain foods or even allergies triggered the behaviors.

Another popular belief was that sugar caused ADHD or made the symptoms worse. However, numerous studies have shown there is no link between sugar consumption and ADHD. Scientists are currently trying to confirm a suggested connection between occurrences of hyperactivity and food additives, such as artificial colors and preservatives, but there are no definitive answers through research studies yet.

Dr. Stanley Greenspan says in his book *Overcoming ADHD* that red dye number 40 can have a visible effect on some children and adults but not affect others. It may be that some people—with and without ADHD—have a "sensitivity" to certain chemicals and artificial substances in foods. It would take some detective work and experimentation to figure out which foods should come out of someone's diet. It is a wise idea to eat as healthfully as possible anyway.

Medication Abuse

Much of the debate surrounding ADHD focuses on the pros and cons of medicating young people. According to an article in the *New York Times*, young adults are the fastest-growing population taking ADHD medications. In one recent year, almost fourteen million prescriptions were written for Americans between twenty and thirty-nine years old. That is more than double the amount written just a few years prior. Many of these are people who have grown up being treated for ADHD while some are newly recognized as having the disorder.

But there are those young adults who do not have ADHD and take stimulant prescriptions. Why would they do this? Some use them for the focus they think they need to study for schoolwork. This abuse is not rare; reports estimate that between 8 and 35 percent of college students take stimulant pills. When stimulants are taken when they are not needed or not taken as directed, patients are more likely to cause harm to their bodies. They can become addicted and even overdose. Large quantities of stimulants operate like a neurotoxin, which mean they act as a poison that can stop the functioning of neurons. Some people have even had psychotic or suicidal tendencies after taking a high dose of stimulants.

Medications are not a good way to cope with problems in life that can be handled in other ways. Abuse of ADHD drugs has become a great problem in recent years.

How do these people get the medications? Some take pills from friends who have ADHD. Giving or receiving medication from someone with a prescription is actually a federal crime. Other people lie when they are being diagnosed. They know what to say to make the doctor think they have ADHD. Since there is no way to objectively test ADHD, the doctor takes them at their word. This was the case with Richard Fee, a young man addicted to Adderall, an

ADHD medication containing amphetamine. A former class president on the path to medical school, Fee killed himself in November 2011 after years of abuse. His story emphasizes the necessity of including therapy along with medication for the treatment of ADHD. The warning signs of his addiction might have been more apparent had Fee been working with a team of professionals. There is no doubt that many with ADHD greatly benefit from stimulant medications when taken as directed. That coupled with therapy can give them normal lives. But stories like that of Richard Fee are reminders that medications are not a quick fix for this complicated disorder.

10 Great Questions to Ask a Therapist

1. How do I tell people I have ADHD?

2. Should people with ADHD be treated any differently?

3. Will my ADHD change with age?

4. What if I do not want special treatment at school?

5. What do I do if I disagree with the treatment my doctor recommends?

6. Do I need medication, or can I be treated effectively without it?

7. Will I become addicted to my medication or experience other side effects?

8. How will I know if my medication is working?

9. How will the medication affect me in the long term?

10. Are there alternative therapies I should try?

Living Well with ADHD

There are many symptoms of ADHD that have a detrimental effect on a young person's lifestyle, making it easy to focus on the negatives of the condition. However, you may be surprised to hear that many people with ADHD share positive, valuable characteristics. For example, unsurprisingly, people with ADHD tend to have a lot of energy. They can channel their liveliness to continuously tackle challenges, while those without that energy may give up. In addition, people with

ADHD usually have a good sense of humor, are often creative, and have an independent streak, too. These qualities can be harnessed to carve out successful careers.

Star Success Stories

Many people have achieved great things while living with ADHD. Some are even in the public eye. Ty Pennington, the famous carpenter and host of the television show *Extreme Makeover: Home Edition*, has struggled with ADHD his whole life. In an interview with the *Huffington Post*, Pennington revealed that he controls the disorder by seeing a psychiatrist and taking small doses of medication when needed. He recalled how the diagnosis hurt his self-esteem growing up but treatment turned his life around. Pennington also advised, "Even if you're on medication, you still have to treat your body properly and take care of yourself."

Singers Justin Timberlake and Solange Knowles both have ADHD.

Besides having ADHD, Justin Timberlake has also revealed he has obsessive-compulsive disorder. Despite these setbacks, he was able to become extremely successful.

Knowles went to two doctors before she believed she had it. "I didn't believe the first doctor who told me," Knowles told Health.com. "I guess I was in denial."

Olympic swimming superstar Michael Phelps was diagnosed with ADHD in fifth grade. He took the medication Ritalin for two years to control his inability to sit still in class, among other problems. Phelps said he later used competitive swimming to utilize his extra energy.

Cammi Granato, an Olympic gold medal–winning hockey player, also believes her ADHD may have helped her in athletics. Granato told the *St. Louis Post-Dispatch*, "It's affected me in positive and negative ways. It's really my worst and best qualities wrapped in one." Many others with ADHD would likely agree with Granato, including chef Jamie Oliver, dancer Karina Smirnoff, and comedian Jim Carrey.

Taking Charge

ADHD has profound effects on people's lives. If you have ADHD, you might feel helpless even if many people are trying to assist you daily. There are certain things that all young people with ADHD can do themselves to be happier and more productive. These are some small ways to take control:

> *Use organizational tools.* Calendars and planners can help you organize and prepare. If you own a smartphone or electronic tablet, many applications are available that can remind you of important events and tasks.

Limit distractions in school and at home. In the classroom, sit in front and away from windows or someplace where classmates, activity, and noise won't divert your attention from the teacher. Talk with your teacher about other ways to avoid getting sidetracked. At home, do your homework away from the computer if possible. If you have to work on the computer, don't have e-mail and instant messaging applications open at the same time. Turn off your phone as well.

Exercise. Exercise has been shown to have a positive effect on young people with ADHD. It can help you feel less restless and more able to concentrate on tasks. This may include taking exercise breaks during long stretches of study.

Talk with friends. Tell your friends about your ADHD. Let them know how it affects some of your actions. However, do not blame bad behavior on ADHD; apologize when needed. This will help strengthen your friendships.

How to Support Someone with ADHD

If you have a brother or sister with ADHD, the best way you can offer support is to learn as much as you can about his or her unique condition. Sometimes it may seem that

Just having someone to talk to about ADHD is extremely helpful in coping with the condition. Many different kinds of support groups are available.

your sibling receives a lot of your parents' attention. You may feel left out or angry, or you may feel anxious and worried. All these emotions are normal. It is important that you talk to your parents about how you feel. You may need some time alone with them every once in a while.

Family therapy can help you, your parents, and your sibling find ways to deal with the stress that accompanies ADHD. Individual therapy may also offer you a safe place to talk about your feelings. A trained counselor can help you establish methods of communicating with your sibling. You can help him or her cope with ADHD just as much as your parents do, just by being patient and listening. There are also support groups, both online and offline, for young people who are siblings of people with ADHD. It can be helpful to talk to other people in your situation.

If you have a friend or classmate with ADHD, keep in mind that he or she is just like you in many ways. ADHD may make people act out, causing others to mock or shun them. People with ADHD are still people, people whose feelings can be deeply hurt. You can support them by sticking up for them in front of bullies and treating them normally.

Into the Future

There is still a lot we do not know about ADHD, but with the amount of people who are living with the disorder, research will focus on finding answers in the years to come. Scientists will try to develop more conclusive tests to diagnose ADHD. They will work to manufacture more effective, nonaddictive medication to minimize the serious side effects of prescription drugs. And finally, research will endeavor to discover the causes of ADHD so as to minimize the risk factors or even prevent the disorder in the future.

Until that day, young people with ADHD must take action to advocate for themselves and for others with the condition. They must take advantage of the many kinds of therapies and interventions available so that they, too, can be examples of success stories.

advocate To support or speak in favor of something or someone.

detrimental Describes something that can cause harm or danger.

divert To draw attention to something else.

gene therapy The treatment of a genetic disease through the insertion of normal or genetically altered genes into cells in order to replace or make up for nonfunctioning or missing genes.

hyperactive Abnormally active, restless, and lacking the ability to concentrate for a length of time.

malnutrition A lack of healthy foods in the diet or an excessive intake of unhealthy foods.

mania Disorder characterized by excessive physical activity, rapidly changing ideas, and impulsive behavior.

neuron A cell that transmits nerve impulses and is the basic unit of the nervous system.

neurotransmitter A chemical that carries messages between different nerve cells or between nerve cells and muscles.

pathologist A scientist who is skilled in identifying the nature, origin, progress, and causes of disease.

preservative Something that provides protection from decay or spoilage.

prevalence The state of being frequent or widespread.

psychotherapy The treatment of mental disorders using mental processes.

psychotic A loss of contact with reality that usually includes false beliefs about what is taking place, as well as seeing or hearing things that are not there.

puberty The life stage in which someone becomes capable of reproduction.

schizophrenia A mental disorder in which it is hard to think clearly, know what is real, have normal emotional responses, and act normally in social situations.

stimulant A drug that produces a temporary increase in functional activity.

stimulus Something that provokes interest.

subjective Something based on opinions or feelings rather than facts or evidence.

unique The only one of its kind.

ADDA (Attention Deficit Disorder Association)
P.O. Box 7557
Wilmington, DE 19803
(800) 939-1019
Web site: http://www.add.org
ADDA offers information on adult and adolescent ADHD
and helps connect local chapters.

ADHD Aware
8 E. Court Street
Doylestown, PA 18901
(215) 348-0550
Web site: http://www.adhdaware.org
Run by and for people with ADHD, ADHD Aware empowers
children, adults, and families living with ADHD.

Canadian ADHD Resource Alliance (CADDRA)
3950 14th Avenue, Suite 604
Markham, ON L3R 0A9
Canada
(416) 637-8583
Web site: http://www.caddra.ca
This is an alliance of ADHD health care professionals who con-
duct research, treat patients, and produce the Canadian
ADHD Practice Guidelines for treating ADHD.

Centre for ADHD Awareness Canada
40 Wynford Drive 304B
Toronto, ON M3C 1J5
Canada
(416) 637 8584

Web site: http://www.caddac.ca

CADDAC is a national, not-for-profit organization that supports those affected by ADHD through education and advocacy.

CHADD (Children and Adults with Attention-Deficit/Hyperactivity Disorder)
8181 Professional Place, Suite 150
Landover, MD 20785
(301) 306-7070
Web site: http://www.chadd.org

CHADD has local chapters throughout the United States. At CHADD's Web site, you can connect with over sixteen thousand members affected by ADHD.

Edge Foundation
2017 Fairview Avenue East, Suite I
Seattle, WA 98102
(888) 718-8886
Web site: https://www.edgefoundation.org

This organization matches teenagers with ADHD with "coaches" that help them succeed in school.

Web Sites

Due to the changing nature of Internet links, Rosen Publishing has developed an online list of Web sites related to the subject of this book. This site is updated regularly. Please use this link to access the list:

http://www.rosenlinks.com/TMH/ADD

Corman, Catherine A., and Edward M Hallowell. *Positively ADD: Real Success Stories to Inspire Your Dreams*. New York, NY: Walker, 2006.

Farrar, Amy. *ADHD*. Minneapolis, MN: Twenty-First Century Books, 2011.

Hammerness, Paul Graves. *ADHD*. Westport, CT: Greenwood Press, 2009.

Jacobs, Carole, and Isadore Wendel. *The Everything Parent's Guide to ADHD in Children: A Reassuring Guide to Getting the Right Diagnosis, Understanding Treatments, and Helping Your Child Focus*. Avon, MA: Adams Media: 2010.

Kennedy, Diane M., Rebecca S. Banks, and Temple Grandin. *Bright Not Broken: Gifted Kids, ADHD, and Autism*. San Francisco, CA: Jossey-Bass, 2011.

Kutscher, Martin L. *ADHD: Living Without Brakes*. Philadelphia, PA: Jessica Kingsley Publishers, 2008.

McIntosh, Kenneth, and Phyllis Livingston. *Youth with Depression and Anxiety: Moods That Overwhelm*. Philadelphia, PA: Mason Crest Publishers, 2008.

Meyers, Karen, Robert N. Golden, and Fred L. Peterson. *The Truth About ADHD and Other Neurobiological Disorders*. New York, NY: Facts On File, 2010.

Petersen, Christine. *Does Everyone Have ADHD? A Teen's Guide to Diagnosis and Treatment*. New York, NY: Franklin Watts, 2006.

Silverstein, Alvin, Virginia B. Silverstein, and Laura Silverstein Nunn. *The ADHD Update: Understanding Attention-Deficit/Hyperactivity Disorder*. Berkeley Heights, NJ: Enslow Publishers, 2008.

Surman, Craig, Tim Bilkey, and Karen Weintraub. *Fast Minds: What to Do If You Have ADHD (or Think You Might)*. New York, NY: Berkley Publishing Group, 2013.

Taylor, Blake E. S. *ADHD & Me: What I Learned from Lighting Fires at the Dinner Table*. Oakland, CA: New Harbinger Publications, 2007.

Timimi, Sami, and Jonathan Leo. *Rethinking ADHD: From Brain to Culture*. New York, NY: Palgrave Macmillan, 2009.

Whitely, Martin. *Speed Up & Sit Still: The Controversies of ADHD Diagnosis and Treatment*. Crawley, WA: UWA Publishing, 2010.

Zager, Karen, Alice K. Rubenstein, Judith Marsden, and Isabelle Delvare. *Handling Difficult Emotions: Anxiety, Depression, and Mood Swings: Psychologists Answer Questions Put to Them by Teenage Girls*. Gallo Manor, South Africa: Awareness Publishing, 2009.

A

ADD and ADHD
  causes of, 10, 16–18, 31–32
  diagnosis of, 21, 22–23
  getting help for, 19–26
  living well with, 35–40
  medications for, 27–34
  myths and facts about, 10
  overview of, 4–9
  symptoms of, 5–6, 11–18, 21
Adderall, 28, 33
American Academy of Pediatrics, 15
antidepressants, 30

C

Carrey, Jim, 37
Centers for Disease Control and
  Prevention (CDC), 7, 8, 27
coexisting disorders, 15–16, 21

D

*Diagnostic and Statistical Manual
  for Mental Disorders* (*DSM*),
  11, 13

F

Fee, Richard, 33–34

G

Granato, Cammi, 37
Greenspan, Dr. Stanley, 32

I

Individualized Education
  Programs (IEPs), 26
Individuals with Disabilities
  Education Act (IDEA), 26

K

Knowles, Solange, 36, 37

L

learning disabilities, 15, 21, 26
Learning Disabilities Association
  of America, 15

M

medication, abuse of, 32–34
multimodal treatment, 23–25, 30

O

Oliver, Jamie, 37
Overcoming ADHD, 32

P

Pennington, Ty, 36
Phelps, Michael, 37

R

Rehabilitation Act of 1973, 26
Ritalin, 28, 37

S

schizophrenia, 6
Smirnoff, Karina, 37
stimulants, 28–29, 30, 33, 34
suicide, 29, 33, 34

T

therapist, 10 great questions to
  ask a, 34
Timberlake, Justin, 36

About the Author

Therese Shea, an author and former educator, has written over one hundred books on a wide variety of subjects. Her most recent have delved into topics such as dementia, physical therapy, and cyberbullying. She holds degrees from Providence College and the State University of New York at Buffalo, and currently resides in Atlanta, Georgia, with her husband, Mark.

Photo Credits